The Art of the Moment

By Véronique Vienne with photographs by Ann Rhoney

The Art of the Moment

SIMPLE WAYS TO GET THE MOST FROM LIFE

Clarkson Potter/Publishers
New York

Text copyright © 2002 by Véronique Vienne
Photographs copyright © 2002 by Ann Rhoney

Published by Clarkson Potter/Publishers, New York, New York.
Member of the Crown Publishing Group, a division of Random House, Inc.
www.randomhouse.com

CLARKSON N. POTTER is a trademark and POTTER and colophon are
registered trademarks of Random House, Inc.

Printed in Singapore

Library of Congress Cataloging-in-Publication Data
Vienne, Véronique.
The art of the moment: simple ways to get the most from life / by Véronique Vienne;
with photographs by Ann Rhoney.—1st ed.
Includes bibliographical references.
1. Quality of life. I. Title.
BF637.C5.V54   2002
158.1—dc21   2002023869

ISBN 0-609-60925-4

10   9   8   7   6   5   4   3   2

First Edition

DEDICATION

To Bill

ACKNOWLEDGMENTS

In the aftermath of September 11, 2001, we all came to understand that every single moment of the day is a gift to be treasured. This book was written as a reminder that the here and now is indeed our most valuable possession, one we share equally with everyone—not only with family and friends, but also with strangers whose presence is as precious as our own.

First, we would like to thank Annetta Hanna for the unfaltering sincerity of her thoughtful comments. Helen Forson Pratt, Seamus Mullarkey, and Marysarah Quinn also gave generous and enlightened advice. And behind the scenes, Teresa Nicholas, Elizabeth Royles, and Caitlin Daniels Israel provided invaluable support.

We are deeply beholden to the people portrayed here, particularly Cathy Raymond, Becky and Doug Scott, Charles Denson, Elizabeth and Allyson Shea, Wendy Silverman, Kathleen Fink, Dorothy Gilliam, Hannah Cohen, Lily Hoffman, Owen Edwards, Dash, Rhonda Rubinstein, and David Peters.

We also want to take this opportunity to acknowledge those who have unwittingly inspired us with their courage and joie de vivre. On Ann's list are Paul and Patricia Rhoney, Mark Rhoney, Claire, Paula, and Colette Rhoney, as well as Sylvia Plachy, Nion McEvoy, Kevin Walz, Anthony Bannon, John Dolan, and Peter Schwartzott. On Véronique's list are Russell Black, Philippe Bourguignon, Dwight and Janice Carter, Bob Ciano, Franny Elder, André Godfrey, Isabel Hoffman, Steven Kelemen, Jeanne Lipsey, Kristin Nicouleau, Frank Stefanich, Alex Streit, and Lloyd Ziff.

CONTENTS

We seek the immediacy of the moment in the
same way flowers seek the sun.

Precious moments often slip by unnoticed. A rainy summer night in a rented beach cottage, a productive afternoon spent cleaning up the yard, a bus ride uptown to visit an old friend—these are the sweet memories we will cherish in hindsight.

But why do we wait for nostalgic flashbacks to appreciate the value of these blissful moments? "Seize the day, put no trust in the morrow!" wrote the Roman poet Horace two millennia ago. Known as *carpe diem* (literally "pluck the day"), his celebrated formula is an exhortation to make the most of what life has to offer. Don't wait for a second chance to get it right. Remember that each time you rest your eyes on a familiar landscape, on a favorite object, or on a beloved face, it is both the first time and the last time because no two days are ever alike.

As you embrace the here and now, don't be surprised if you suddenly feel lucky—lucky to be blessed with a good mind, lucky to have friends who love you for who you are, lucky to be living in such an interesting time. The ultimate gift of the moment is a deep sense of gratitude for simply being alive.

This book will inspire you not to postpone enjoying the small fleeting pleasures that are yours for the taking, as you prepare a meal, as you cross the street, as you talk on the phone, or as you try to remember where you left your keys.

In a world where there is never quite enough time, just take a few minutes to flip through these pages. You might find that, as brief as it is, the present moment is always the right time to get the most from life.

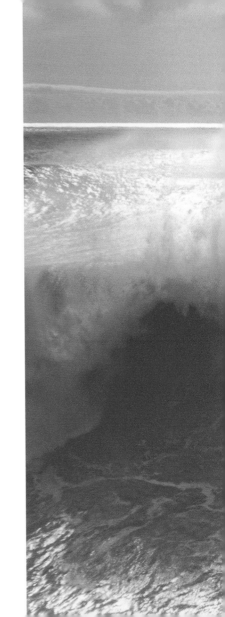

the art of joy

n this earth, you get a prize for just showing up. Joy is your birthright. Now and then, all through your life, you can expect to feel lighthearted, often when you least expect it, and sometimes even when it's not appropriate.

But *c'est la vie!* Joie de vivre, as the French call it, is pure joy of living—a form of cheerfulness that ignores rationalization.

You don't even have to be happy to experience a spell of levity. It can happen when you are cranky, tired, sad, or worried. All it takes is a small inducement and the next thing you know, you are glad to be alive and grateful for the love you feel in your heart.

Maybe an old man with a kindly face sat next to you on the train and smiled at you. Or perhaps you just tried on a fabulous pair of boots. Or, possibly, you were taken aback by the glorious sight of fall foliage illuminated against a stormy gray sky. Suddenly, for a fleeting moment, you are emotionally fulfilled, at peace with yourself at last.

Personal achievements or successes are seldom the reason why you experience this particular form of happiness. In fact, the inexplicable nature of joie de vivre is a major part of its appeal. Mysteriously, you become enthused by the miraculous spectacle of ordinary life unfolding right in front of you.

You can be taken by surprise by a burst of elation even though you may be distressed about a situation at work, uneasy about an upcoming decision, or recovering from a sentimental breakup. All you need to feel joyful is an unexpected sunny day, an admiring glance from someone across the room, a line in a poem, or an invitation to catch up over lunch from a former boss.

This gift of instant joy is so much a part of the human experience that even the most cynical among us are not immune to it. Did you ever notice the way alarmists carry on with their pessimistic views? One can only assume that they find pleasure in it. And, to be honest, you and I sometimes derive a certain romantic satisfaction from our most indulgent bouts of self-pity.

Every so often, like it or not, our brain is washed over with feel-good chemicals—

nature's reward to us for putting up with the world's troubles.

So instead of trying to cheer up when in truth you have no reason to be happy, give yourself a break. Don't put a brave smile on your face. Instead, look around and be open to what's out there. People-watching can ease your misery faster than swallowing pills. Joie de vivre, after all, was invented by the same people who gave us street fashion and terrace cafés.

But you don't have to go to Paris to find joie de vivre. Public places offer great opportunities to anyone in need of instant joy. Right on your block, pet stores, hair-dressers, and pastry shops may provide serendipitous encounters likely to lift the corners of your mouth. Other rewarding venues include art museums, farmers' markets, picnic grounds, roadside diners, hotel lobbies, aquariums, and public libraries.

You never know when you are going to be overwhelmed with a sweet effervescence. This emotion could be triggered by the look of expectation on the face of a dog when its owner says "Let's go." By a teenage boy holding a WELCOME HOME, DAD sign at the airport. Or by a little girl in her Sunday best sitting pretty on a suitcase at a bus stop.

Beware. Feeling blue is never an excuse for passing on a chance to feel joy.

WHAT MONEY
CAN'T BUY

❀

Money can buy some happiness—how about a Jaguar in the garage?—but no amount of cash can buy the gift of joy. No one can pay for something that life grants for free. "Bliss is the same in subject and in king," said English poet Alexander Pope.

You are blessed, whether or not you think you deserve it.

Still, most of us will postpone appreciating life's fleeting rewards until we feel that we have enough money in the bank.

We can't truly enjoy sleeping late on a weekday unless it's a national holiday.

We would feel guilty cutting short a business trip to go fishing—only rich folks can take the time to goof off.

And leaving our cell phone at home when going on a five-day vacation is out of the question.

If you stop to think about it, it doesn't make sense: We save money in order to feel secure enough to enjoy the things that money can't buy. Why can't we give ourselves permission to take what's freely given? Why do we feel that we have to purchase our own joy?

Go ahead, make excuses for not being able to take it easy more often. The mortgage. The tuition. The taxes. The car payments. Not to mention the old boiler in the basement. Fair enough. Yet, as urgent as it is, financial pressure is not the only explanation for our constant toiling. In reality, we believe that we have to earn the right to have a good time. When it comes to feeling joyful, we don't want to accept any handouts from benevolent gods.

But don't blame Puritan ethics for your inability to bask in the pleasure of being alive. Twenty-five centuries ago in ancient Greece, the philosopher Epicurus was already championing a joie de vivre exempt from the trappings of opulence. In the refined school of hedonism he created in Athens, water was the usual drink and plain barley bread was shared among the students.

Even if you have everything—and can afford the best there is—discover how satisfying it can be to live simply, yet generously.

Try, for instance, to lend interest-free money to friends who need it—regardless of their ability to repay you promptly. Even better, if you can, just give the funds away without a second thought. Surprisingly, divesting oneself of extra cash can be a gleeful experience. With less change in your pocket, you'll feel liberated. Perhaps you'll do something silly, like eat cotton candy, go to a movie matinee, or sit down under a tree with a good book.

The Gift of Forgetfulness

"Happiness? That's nothing more than health and a poor memory," said Nobel Prize winner Albert Schweitzer. A doctor, musician, humanitarian, and philosopher, he reinvented himself time and time again.

Enjoy your memory lapses—they make each moment a second-to-none occurrence.

- Be here now: Live as if you won't remember tomorrow what you did today.

- Be carefree: Forget what you think you know and let the world take you by surprise.

- Be blessed: Forget what you want but enjoy what you get.

- Be popular: Forget to point out that you were right in the first place.

- Be memorable: Take for granted that most folks will forget what you said but will always remember how you made them feel.

- Be generous: Between friends, forget what must be forgotten.

- Be truthful: Don't lie and you won't have to remember a thing.

- Be forgiving: Forget the age of anyone over 35.

- Be modest: Forget to mention your accomplishments.

- Be ready: This is it. The rest is but a memory.

Make the most of what comes and the least of what goes.

the art of
improvisation

cting on impulse makes you feel young. It's the ultimate antiage treatment. What the heck! Decide to throw a party on the spur of the moment. Make a funny off-the-cuff comment. Have an impromptu conversation with the kid next door. How old you are is inversely proportional to your spontaneity quotient.

This is why a split-second decision is a thrill at

any age, as exciting to the wide-eyed toddler who decides to jump into a pool feet-first as it is to the retired schoolteacher who walks into a travel agency one day and buys a round trip ticket to New Zealand.

To improvise is to extemporize—from *ex tempore* in Latin; it means to do something "out of time," something not dated, never obsolete, always new.

By definition, there are no instructions for improvisation—you wing it every time. But even though you are not bound by any rules, you are not totally on your own. Each inspired move you make is guided by the invisible hand of the present tense.

Improvisation is the child of the moment. It thrives under the benevolent glance of the instant. "I don't search, I find," said Picasso, commenting on the fact that, for him at least, creativity was not a lengthy process of trial and error but the discovery of a hidden reality tucked away in the immediacy of the here and now.

For the rest of us, improvisation comes as the result of a period of fumbling. What's for dinner? you may wonder. You open the refrigerator and your mind goes blank as you stare into the glaring light of your frosty larder. If you are in a potluck mood, you'll be able to turn a frozen pizza into a gourmet dish. But not before you scare up a forlorn onion, a dash of paprika, a cup of plain yogurt, a sprig of wilted parsley, and a teaspoon of ground cumin.

Then, impetuously, you will juggle all of the ingredients, and as if by magic, you will turn the slim pickings into a speedy Middle Eastern feast.

All artists, from chefs to painters, from poets to composers, must struggle to achieve this creative breakthrough.

But take heart. With the exception of Picasso, most geniuses can't wing it either.

Before inventing the lightbulb Thomas

Spontaneity increases with practice.

Edison floundered for years, coming up with hundreds of useless patents. Charles Darwin was no quick thinker: his contribution to science came at the end of tedious pondering sessions. And Abraham Lincoln scribbled ideas on scraps of paper before shaping them into memorable speeches.

Even fashion designers, who are supposed to be "inspired," agonize over their creations. The length of the sleeves is all wrong. Get rid of those shoes. Add a scarf. No, take it away. Try the boots. How about a belt? They fuss and fuss until, miraculously, the muse takes over. Only then will the clothes look young, unfettered, effortless.

Jazz musicians have made an art of live improvisation. But you don't have to be a horn player or a blues singer to emulate Louis Armstrong. You, too, can play it by ear: All you have to do is listen. Spontaneity springs from a quiet place deep inside

yourself, and if you pay attention, you can find its source.

When you are on a roll—when the impromptu feels like second nature—the voices of self-doubt are silenced at last. Improvising then is as easy as singing along to your favorite tune.

BEST-LAID PLANS

✤

You can't leave it all to chance. If only to tempt fate, you have to map out the foreseeable future. But take it for granted that your best-laid plans will conflict with your good fortune. When it rains, it pours.

As you are about to close a deal on your first home, you'll get a chance to spend a year in Rome on a generous scholarship. When at long last the plumber decides to come fix your sewage system, a crew from the local television station will show up to interview you. And the day you are scheduled to have cosmetic surgery, you will get two free orchestra tickets to the season's premiere at the opera house. Opportunity knocks at the least opportune moment. The best invitations always come when you have previous engagements.

You don't want the thought of crossing off items on your calendar to be the source of most of your pleasures in life. Don't let the golden moment fly. Don't consult your Palm Pilot as if you were reading the lines on the palm of your hand.

To prevent future concerns from spoiling the present moment, make a list of all the things you'd like to do in the next couple of years and hang it on the wall next to your desk. The longer the list, the better. Fake it if you must. String the words together as if you were writing the lyrics of a cool jazz tune.

Reframe family pictures
Learn aikido
Sharpen kitchen knives
Support public television
Read *The Little Prince* aloud
Make a dentist appointment
Visit relatives in Copenhagen
Buy a new bathing suit
Only drink great wine

In the coming months, you'll strike out some entries, add new ones, highlight others, and scribble notes all over them. Let the piece of paper get as dog-eared as a Tibetan prayer flag fluttering in the wind. Place a small vase of dried flowers under the list and tack a favorite postcard next to it. As this little shrine gathers dust, watch the future become the past in front of your very eyes.

Live in the present. Be prepared to improvise.

Surprise, surprise:
Looking good makes you feel smart.

How to Be Suddenly Chic

Unlike elegance, which requires taste and distinction, chicness is a matter of vitality and verve. You can always pull it off at the last minute if you have the wherewithal to improvise.

1. Have panache: Don't shuffle as you walk. Lengthen your steps by a half-inch and you'll gain three inches in stature.

2. Put on the ritz: Wear clothes with an attitude. Find the body language that enhances the cut and style of your outfit. Be in sync with your cropped jacket, your funnel neck, and your raglan sleeves.

3. Show some flair: Flaunt your big jewelry when you are in a great mood. Wear bright lipstick with a very short haircut. Stay away from black clothes if you have a pet. And don't sport dainty shoes on public transportation.

4. Express yourself with élan: Use colloquial expressions to show that you don't take yourself too seriously. Keep phone conversations short and sweet. And say "Don't ask" or "Go figure" rather than launch into long explanations.

5. Display your savoir faire: Smile as you hold the door for others. Be sure to compliment the chef. And always have a kind word for people with old dogs.

6. Be swell: When in doubt, err on the plus side. Overtip, bend over backward, ham it up, burn the candle at both ends, spoil children, expect too much, and subjugate the other sex with your charm.

the art of wonder

f all the gifts you received at birth, your ability to behold the beauty of the world is the most precious. With your eyes, you can conjure up soul-stirring scenes and sights. With your ears, you can become aware of distant songs and haunting melodies. With your touch and taste, you can discover and savor realms of infinite delights. Your senses are endowed with an occult

The breeze will carry away every
shimmering time bubble.

power that should be the envy of every wizard and sorcerer from Anaheim to Oz.

The magic wand that can spread fairy dust on everything you hear, touch, and see is called attention.

The wonderful thing about attention is its fluidity. Like water, it flows effortlessly from its original source somewhere in your mind. Even though most of the time your attention just ripples over the surface of things, giving them an agreeable sheen, it can also penetrate into the smallest nooks and crannies, highlighting minute details under the magnifying glass of its liquid lens.

Your attention can allow you to see the beauty of a vacant lot, of an overpass, of a parking lot, even of a blank wall. It can also reveal to you what no one else notices: the sound of leaves rustling in the breeze, the brave determination of an old lady crossing a busy intersection, the colors of wet umbrellas dancing above a crowd.

In contrast, when you are self-involved (when you are held hostage by your internal dialogue) everyday reality feels quite banal. If you are in a distracted mood, everything is a blur, a drone, a blah—a so-what.

You are on your way to meet a loved one, rehearsing in your mind what you are going to say. You are in a fancy restaurant, scrutinizing the lengthy menu. You just got home and are checking your voice mail. Absorbed in your thoughts, you are not mindful of what's going on around you. Why should you be? As far as you are concerned, nothing is happening.

But wait a minute! Are you sure that nothing is happening? Or could it be that what you assume is "nothing" is, in fact, the lull that precedes a really important event.

☙ The quiet in a church before the bride says "I do."

The suspense before the curtain rises.

The pause before the first applause.

The breath you take before signing
your name on a lease.

The tap on your shoulder before
you turn around.

The deep sigh of a baby before
she drifts to sleep.

The hush that precedes the first
notes of a symphony.

Before an orchestra can start playing, the conductor raises his baton to create what's called in musical language an anacrusis—a silent upbeat. In the same way, every moment can be interpreted as a silent upbeat, as a brief interval between what was and what is still to be.

To reveal the wonder of life, all you need to do is imagine yourself raising a conductor's baton. With this mental gesture, you call the world to your atten-tion. Instantaneously, everything comes into focus: the book on the table, the pot on the stove, the flowers in the vase.

This is a magical moment, a mystical point of departure like the "once upon a time" that begins all myths and fables.

IN PRAISE OF THE SHORT ATTENTION SPAN

&

Attention, like water, is a playful element. It doesn't like to be contained for very long. Rather than try to force yourself to be on the lookout, practice following your attention wherever it wants to go.

One minute you are looking up at rooftops, the next you notice that your shoelace is untied. You remember to make a phone call as you bend over to hug your child. You lose your train of thought in the middle of a sentence when you notice water stains on the piano. Don't worry. You are not attention-deficient. On the contrary, you are remarkably aware of the ballet of your vigilance.

To convince yourself that what you mistook for a weakness is, in fact, a talent for observation, pick a random moment in your day and decide to track what you see, hear, and think for the next sixty seconds. Life is ready whenever you are. "We live to discover beauty/All else is a form of waiting," wrote the Lebanese-American poet Kahlil Gibran.

Don't wait too long. Embrace the gift of life as soon, and as often, as you can. Keep in mind, though, that a walk down the street in a quiet residential neighborhood can be particularly rewarding.

Watch it all unfold: a father pushing a stroller with one hand, an open window framing a bespectacled gentleman holding a watering can, and then, out of the blue, the intrusion of your unresolved concern for a friend who recently moved to Japan.

Fifteen seconds later you are back in the present, just in time to catch a glimpse of a red car turning the corner. That's when you remember that you have to get a refill for one of your prescriptions. Then, in the far corner of a parking lot, you notice a young couple practicing fox-trot moves to the music coming from their minivan's radio.

The wonder of the world is yours to witness. A round-the-clock production, your life is a spectacle you can enjoy for the price of one admission. You can come and go as you like, without restrictions. From time to time you may be called on to play a bit part in it, in which case you get a closer look at the scenery and the action.

You don't have to travel far to see the beauty of the world. It is always there, within reach, at the other end of the notoriously short leash of your attention.

The Kodak Moment

Before the invention of photography, people relied on their visual memory to preserve the wonder of the moment. Today your camera can record for posterity an instant so brief—$^1/_{125}$ of a second—that you can't even see it.

But what you can't see, you can feel. When taking photographs of people, be ready to click the shutter at that invisible picture-perfect moment.

- Don't take pictures straightaway. Just walk around with your camera. Sit down for a chat. Make everyone feel comfortable.

- Don't hide behind the lens. Let people see your face as much as possible. Talk to them while you shoot. Don't be shy. Don't be pushy.

- Capture the ephemeral quality of the hour. If you can, take pictures early in the morning, when the light is new, or late in the day, when the last rays of the sun are fading. Avoid the harsh midday light: Never shoot outdoors during lunchtime.

- Don't ask people to stand still. If it's a group portrait, make sure you have enough film left in your camera to take pictures at the end, when everyone thinks it's over. That's when they'll relax, laugh, and hug.

- Press the shutter just a split second before—or after—something happens. If you observe people closely, you'll know when their mood is about to change. That's the decisive moment.

- Don't try to get it all in the picture. Partial images are more evocative, and look more real, than wide-angle tableaux.

A camera is a mousetrap for the here and now.

the art of intuition

You are at the center of a formidable information network. Moment by moment a sixth sense keeps you updated on your inner state, your thoughts, and your feelings. You can instantly know everything there is to know about yourself.

Whether or not we choose to decipher them, brief messages are fired off all the time just below

Crack open the door of your intuition
and eavesdrop on your silent thoughts.

the surface of our conscious perceptions. Researchers believe that, on average, four such messages pass through our cortex every minute, half of them less than five seconds long.

Almost instantly, upon meeting someone, we receive a complete report on how the encounter has affected our mood. As the situation evolves, we are alerted in case a new development is likely to annoy us, excite us, or comfort us.

At family gatherings, alarm bells go off to warn you when a sibling is about to push your buttons. At business meetings, an inner voice keeps tabs on whom you can trust. At the breakfast table, a red flag goes up as you are about to reach for that second doughnut. And when a friend calls you to complain about her husband, you get a funny feeling that the real problem is her relationship with her mom.

"I knew it!" you say when you dis-cover, usually too late, that you had a hunch all along that something was wrong.

Trust your intuition. Don't let your reason get the upper hand, as it usually does, and silence your premonitions. A secret envoy is trying to tell you something: Don't discard the privileged information that's yours and yours alone.

What's unique about this particular form of self-knowledge is its immediacy. No painful soul-searching is involved. No session on the couch. No twelve-step program. You get just-the-facts-ma'am—the plain unvarnished truth delivered directly to you by the express messenger of your unconscious.

Even though most intuitive signals are designed to keep us out of harm's way, others simply record our involuntary reactions to the world around us. Often we catch ourselves smiling unintentionally, barely aware of the cause of our levity—a child's first steps, a dog wagging its tail, the shape of a cloud, or spring in the air.

But if you assume, as you should, that you indeed know all there is to know about yourself, you have to assume as well that everyone else is in the same situation. Look around: the world is full of people who are as perceptive and well informed as you are. If they pretend to be clueless, it's only to make life simpler for everyone.

If the lady behind the counter takes too long counting your change, take for granted that she knows exactly what you are thinking, even though you are trying not to show your annoyance.

Make no mistake, the politician shaking your hand is well aware of the fact that you are trying to evaluate his honesty and sincerity.

And no one on the receiving end of an effusive compliment is ever fooled. "Oh my God, you look fabulous—you lost a lot of weight" is usually interpreted as a signal that it's time to go on a diet.

The next time you walk down a crowded street, picture in your mind the complex flow of information that's passing between people. Visualize this exchange of perceptions as a moving stream that's carrying you along. Notice how buoyant you feel. The awareness we all share is our safety net: it is the guardian angel who watches over us.

THE DEVIL'S ADVOCATE

❖

Intuition, we presume, is divine. To "divine" means to perceive intuitively. We experience intuition as a supernatural event, as a spiritual bolt of lightning that short-circuits our rational mind.

Be still! Your unconscious is trying to talk to you!

In contrast, reason is suspected of being devilishly clever. Demonizing the mind is an old tradition, going all the way back to the Bible. Indeed, the Serpent is portrayed as a skilled debater who deceives Eve with fallacious arguments. In Christian folklore, the Devil is called the Clever One, the Mischievous One, or the Trick-ster. And today, even though we celebrate reason, we still hold the brain responsible for our darkest impulses. Criminal behaviors are often interpreted as mental disorders.

Admittedly, our reason has an irresistible need to be the devil's advocate. It loves to argue for the sake of argument.

Case in point, the mercenary philosophers in ancient Greece who became famous for arguing on behalf of anyone willing to pay their price. Called Sophists, these shrewd orators gave rhetoric a bad name. Today the word *sophism* is used to describe an argument that's plausible yet deceptive.

No doubt, in the West, we have neglected intuitive understanding and given the intellect too much power. But inspired by Eastern thinkers, and by the latest findings of advanced biochemistry, we are now coming to terms with the fact that the body has an intelligence of its own. What we call gut feelings are evidence of a communication system between our conscious and unconscious perceptions.

Your throat dries up to let you know that you should keep your mouth shut.

You get a funny feeling in the pit of your stomach the minute you fall in love.

And before you can figure out what's bothering you, you scratch your head and wrinkle your brow.

Gaining insight into oneself is an all-embracing, head-to-toe process that involves the body as well as the mind. It requires that you eavesdrop on your thoughts, your feelings, and your physical sensations. More than just an internal voice, your intuition is an overall presence—a well-informed oracle who dwells within you.

This oracle is as earthly as it is divine. The celebrated dictum "Know thyself" was written on the portal of the Greek temple at Delphi, originally dedicated to Mother Earth. People traveled there from all over the ancient world to consult a medium who spoke from a cell, deep under the shrine. Even though the temple at Delphi is a ruin today, its oracle has not been silenced. She still speaks from the depths, from a place buried within each of us.

Try to look at the world as if you were a cat.

What You Know

Sometimes you need to deliberate before reaching a decision. But there are instances when the choices are clear and you know at once what to do. Trust yourself: you are wise, indeed, when you decide...

...to think about it in the shower

...to start from scratch

...to wait till morning

...to eat fish at night

...to keep a secret

...to ask a question

...to let it go

...to turn off the TV

...to register to vote

...to be quiet and listen

...to stay home because you are tired

...to go the distance

...to dress up for the occasion

...to keep a low profile

...to get a massage

...to reread a book

There is a sage in all of us.

the art of poise

Arriving late on the scene is often an advantage. Who wants to be the first person at a party, for instance? The guests of honor are usually the last to walk in. Sometimes it's best to be patient and hold back long enough to let others take the lead and get the ball rolling.

Yet we all have a tendency to rush ahead, no matter what, as if to make up for lost time. As mem-

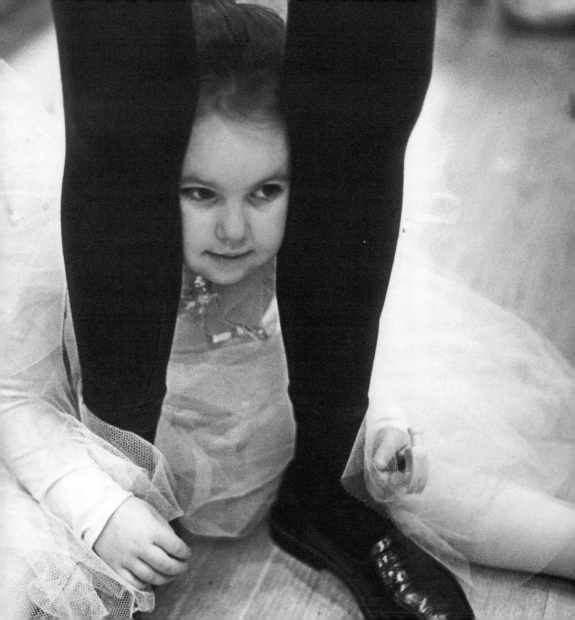

bers of the youngest species on the planet—only fifty thousand years old—we probably feel that we have a lot of catching up to do. Imagine, worms and shellfish have a four-thousand-*million*-year advance over us.

In spite of their handicap, human beings have made extraordinary progress in a very short time. Late bloomers that we are, we gained the upper hand over other creatures by using our brains instead of our teeth and claws.

But let's not get cocky. Our ability to wait and ponder is still key to our development and survival. To slow us down, wise ancestors invented civility. More than a code of social graces, rules of politeness have a moderating effect on our behavior. Each *if you please* and *would you mind,* each *I beg your pardon* and *I am terribly sorry,* stall us just long enough to temper our ever-present impatience. Without poise and composure, we lose our evolutionary advantage!

So take a deep breath and exhale slowly as you utter the words that proper etiquette requires. Your deliberate enunciation is your first line of defense against the dangers of reckless improvidence. In the process you will become a connoisseur of the moment.

We give children the gift of poise when we demand that they knock before entering, when we insist they listen before they speak, and when we tell them to wait for everyone to be seated before starting a meal.

If, for instance, you were taught in kindergarten not to interrupt a conversation, you've learned to wait for your turn. You know your time will come. You don't have to have it all right now—you are probably in less of a hurry to keep up with the Joneses. You can admire a colleague's talent without wanting to emulate her on the spot. You can marvel at cutting-edge technology yet feel no compulsion to buy

Poise is a balancing act between courage and caution.

the latest upgrade. And you can appreciate the craftsmanship of a custom-fitted suit while sporting off-the-rack clothes with grace and flair.

Of necessity, perhaps, you don't expect everything to be perfect. In fact, you have a soft spot in your heart for slightly faded bouquets, Paris in the rain, old sweaters, dripping candles, moss-covered walls, and kids who can't spell.

"Rome wasn't built in one day," you like to say.

And if you had to draw up a short list of what's really urgent, the first thing you'd write down would be: "Find a little more time to be with friends."

Patience is a virtue, says the proverb. But what no one tells you is that you don't need a lot of patience to make a huge difference. A little less haste goes a long way. When you don't give in to the temptation of hurrying, you suddenly feel that you have all the time in the world.

Don't rush; just sashay down a long hallway and the walls and ceiling seem to recede. Get up slowly from your chair after a good dinner and the pleasure of the meal lingers with you for hours. Wait to be the last person out of a crowded elevator and don't be surprised if you feel like a country gentleman giving his guests a tour of his imposing estate.

THE ROLE OF LUXURY

❖

Like polite behavior, luxurious objects are haste inhibitors. Their sensuous texture, fragile aspect, and rare provenance give you pause.

Throw a fur-trimmed cashmere stole over your silk lamé gown and notice how you walk with grace! Order luscious food at a three-star restaurant and watch how you take small bites! Drink coffee from a delicate porcelain cup and see how slowly you lift the demitasse in the air!

Luxury has a calming effect on our psyche. Yes, the rich are different—they can't just swallow their food and run. In the meantime, if you and I ever need a reason to splurge on occasional luxuries, here it is: Unlike tranquillizers or chain-smoking, diamonds, taffeta, and caviar are not addictive.

Today a visit to a spa is the next best thing to a stay at Versailles. Diamond tiaras may be way out of your price range, but a great scalp massage can make you feel like a million dollars. You may not be able to afford silk sheets, but you can always sink into a bubble bath. And even though you may never make an entrance in a Dior evening gown, you can wrap yourself in a big fluffy towel and step out of your bathroom in full glory.

Cultivate small luxuries, particularly if you have a tendency to fret and fidget. Discipline your restless soul not with hair shirts but with alpaca robes, chiffon scarves, velvet slippers.

Or, if your prefer, develop your calm and confidence by collecting well-designed objects such as handmade Japanese bowls, ergonomic chairs, or high-tech eyeglasses. Each time you handle these things, take pleasure in their craftsmanship. This is no trivial pursuit. On the contrary, truly appreciating the quality of a luxury item could be the spiritual highlight of your day.

The greatest luxury, of course, is free time. In the past, there was plenty of it. You could always reserve an hour for reflection in the middle of the day. It used to be called a *coffee break, déjeuner, siesta,* or *high tea,* depending on the country you were in.

Nowadays, every single minute of your waking life is accounted for. But don't let this deter you. Just earmark fifteen percent of your schedule for "revisions and improvements." Use this time allowance to turn off your phone and close your door.

All you need to do is sit still and wait. Yes, wait. "How do I work? I grope," said Einstein. Poise and patience offers creative solutions to those who don't know how or why.

Let It Go Without Saying

People will listen to you patiently if they can hear a pin drop while you talk. In public speaking, silence is an important component of eloquence. If you want to be heard, stand tall, speak slowly—and don't say it all.

- Think of talking as putting an end to your silence.

- Give people time to look at your face before you open your mouth.

- Whet their curiosity: Wait one extra second before speaking.

- Say what you want to say as if it has just occurred to you.

- To dramatize what you are going to say next, exhale, look at your audience— and stop moving your hands.

- Don't feel obliged to spell out every detail.

- Share your thoughts by asking questions. When you want to recap, for instance, say "So, why am I telling you this?"

- To make an important point, slow down enough to listen to your own voice.

- Before your closing statement, let the room grow quiet for a second.

- And remember: "What is said is the least part of the oration" (Ralph Waldo Emerson).

Words are pebbles on a still surface.

the art of
adventure

ne day, while wait-
ing for a friend at the local train station, you bump
into a long-lost cousin who offers you a great job in
Singapore. You move there and rent an apartment
next door to a man who used to be Elvis Presley's
butler. A year later, on a business trip to Memphis,
you visit Graceland and fall in love with the tour
guide. On your honeymoon you go to Paris, where

Wherever you are, it's the right spot and the right time.

your new brother-in-law happens to manage a three-star restaurant. Next thing you know you are sitting in front of an *escalope*

de foie gras de canard à l'orange et au pain d'épices, wondering which fork to use.

If novelists wrote stories as serendipitous as real life, they'd never get published. "Your book doesn't make any sense!" the editor would say. "Readers don't want long-winded narratives that drift aimlessly!"

But truth is stranger than fiction. Most of us live real lives that mock the cardinal rules of creative writing. Our actions never follow a neat plot line. Instead, we digress and wander, at the mercy of coincidences that always seem to derail our best-laid plans. Contrary to what some historians would have us believe, a rendezvous with destiny is a rare thing among human beings.

There is only one type of story that can imitate real life and still find an audience. It is the epic adventure story, a unique genre in literature. Adventure stories don't need a plot. Unlike murder mysteries, thrillers, or tales of love and revenge, there is no cause-and-effect relationship in these long narratives—only turns of fortune that sweep the hero from exotic location to exotic location with no rhyme or reason.

With odysseys as convoluted as Ulysses' journey, adventure stories keep us in suspense with a succession of unpredictable events. One thing always leads to another. Readers are more interested in knowing what, when, and where than in finding out why.

It's the same thing in life. What happens *next* is more compelling than what happens in the end, because every ending is also a beginning. Leaving home coincides with embarking on a new life. Quitting a job is an opportunity to move on. Tying the knot gives you a chance to start a family. And so the story goes on and on and on forever, each dramatic denouement marking a new genesis.

Experience life as an adventure by resisting the temptation to explain everything. Don't waste your time wondering why men are afraid of commitment, why you have to learn the rules in order to break them, or why the line in which you are standing is always the slow one.

Abstain from using the word *because* to justify your actions. In particular, never say "because I love you," "because it's good for you," "because I was told," or "because I need the job."

Be careful when assigning causes and effects to events you don't clearly understand. Lame excuses include: childhood traumas, planetary movements, caffeine side effects, Nostradamus, the government, hormones, the weather, sibling rivalry, violence on television, the economy, Puritan ethics, and western civilization.

In other words, don't expect events in your life to fit a ready-for-prime-time script. Rest assured that were you to become famous, your self-appointed biographers would lose sleep trying to figure out your internal motivations. No, let your life be the epic poem it is. Embrace each moment on its own merit, one at a time, in the sequence in which it happens.

Be the adventurous one.

Go to Singapore (don't miss the Bukit Timah rain forest).

Walk in the footsteps of John Muir from Yosemite Valley to Nevada.

Buy a house in the charming village of Lencois, a two-day drive from Brasilia.

Sign up for a class in photography at the Arles Photography Festival in Provence.

Leave to others the task of figuring out why.

HAPPY ACCIDENTS

✣

Welcome unexpected interruptions for they are often the lead-ins for happy accidents. People who know how to take risks are not afraid of life's annoying setbacks. When things go wrong, instead of backtracking they forge ahead, prodded on by their curiosity.

They have good reasons to be intrigued. The wheel of fortune is set in motion by a mechanism that owes more to the quantum field theory than to Newton's laws of physics. Ask happily married couples how they first met, for instance, and they will tell you long stories involving last-minute cancelations, speeding tickets, stolen passports, long lines, and flat tires in the rain.

Challenge your most simplistic assumptions about cause and effect. Regard small accidents as evidence that you have entered an invisible electromagnetic field that doesn't respond to the gravitational pull of everyday reasoning.

If you get fired from your job the day you were planning to sign a lease for a new apartment, take for granted that this is your lucky day: A year from now you could be selling your first novel for a substantial advance.

If you break a leg the day you were leaving for China on a guided tour of the Yangtze River gorges, you can almost be sure that the emergency-room physician will turn out to be your future spouse's best friend.

If you spill your coffee on the sofa while reaching for the phone, don't be surprised if your caller is from the MacArthur Foundation offering you a grant to pursue your artistic inclinations.

Last but not least, if you lock your keys inside your car, don't curse under your breath. Instead, thank the heavens for reminding you that life is full of surprises. It's not a prepaid trip to a known destination but an exciting journey with twists and turns you could never have predicted.

Expect the Unexpected

Even though there is no telling what will happen next, you can be prepared for it if you know what to take along on your personal journey. Here is a list of items you'll want to pack before heading down the sinuous path of life.

- A solid value system
  (Beware of little white lies.)

- Three quotes from wise people
  (Example: "True generosity means accepting ingratitude."
  —Coco Chanel)

- Photographs of loved ones
  (Include a picture of yourself as a child.)

- A sense of humor
  (There are only three rules to life. But no one knows what they are.)

- A white handkerchief
  (To clean your glasses; to wipe a baby's drool; to wave good-bye)

- One reliable manual skill
  (Sewing, cooking, ironing, welding, fixing things, or playing the piano)

- A second language
  (Spanish, Korean, Italian, Russian, or French)

You will also need to take along personal items you can use for impromptu gifts: a scarf, a charm bracelet, a book, a pen, a wool cap, a locket, or a pair of socks.

Luck is what happens when you are prepared.

the art of love

he gallant admirer who never fails to bring flowers for his date is not as irresistible as the dashing suitor who throws his coat, his gloves, and his hat on the sofa before opening his arms to hold his lover in a passionate embrace.

If you are offering your heart in earnest, don't come bearing gifts. You can't hug—or be hugged—when your hands are full. The body language of love

is the body language of availability. Greet true romance empty-handed.

When two people are in love, they might as well be on a deserted island. The world of mundane concerns ceases to exist. It is a moment of truth of unfettered simplicity and grace—a moment free from need and want.

Lost in the other person's gaze, you are safe. Uncross your arms. Stop fussing with your hair. Take your hands out of your pockets. Put away your cell phone. Don't clutch your notebook or your bag. Unbutton your jacket. Remove your sunglasses. Let down your defenses—make way for what's still to come.

Worrying about exchanging gifts would spoil the moment. "Love's gift cannot be given, it waits to be accepted," wrote the Bengali philosopher Rabindranath Tagore. Gifts always carry with them furtive obligations. Spare your beloved the burden of your expectations. Instead, stand with arms dangling and chest exposed, ready to accept without reserve and without recourse the verdict of his or her heart.

What's true in courtship is also true in friendship. Too much solicitude can clutter an amiable relationship. The globe-trotting fellow who always comes back from his trips with trinkets and souvenirs for you is probably not as welcome in your home as the penniless bachelor who invites himself for dinner with a bold promise to do the dishes.

And even though there is no greater joy than bestowing gifts on children, it's a pleasure one should reserve for special occasions. The well-meaning aunt who always shows up at the door with toys gets to be a nuisance after a while; in the meantime, Grandpa, who never brings anything on his visits but who makes the kids laugh by wiggling his ears, is their favorite grown-up.

When you love, giving is an act of surrender. Practically, it means that you have to give in, give over, or give up. In other words, you have to be willing to go against your own resistance.

An attentive husband, for instance, knows that whenever his wife asks him to take out the trash, his first impulse is to say "Yes, dear"—and not do it. So every time she makes a trivial household demand on him (walk the dog, put away his shoes, empty the dishwasher), he notes the familiar resistance welling up in him. That's his cue. He jumps to his feet. "He that gives quickly gives twice," said Cervantes. The author of *Don Quixote* was chivalrous, indeed. But what is love if not a foolishly impractical venture?

A romantically inclined wife will also forsake her own comfort, particularly when she most resents it. The thing that annoys her about her companion is the way he falls apart when the sink is clogged or the car won't start. So be it. When disaster strikes, she rushes to his side with a screwdriver, a flashlight, and a sponge—even though her nail polish is not quite dry.

Treat daily nuisances as you would Cupid's arrows. Don't recoil or roll your eyes when you feel the sting of irritation. Instead, treat each occasion to surrender as a timely reminder that the greatest gift you can give to someone you love is the gift of unconditional acceptance.

SOCIAL   GRACES

✤

We all know the precepts love thy neighbor and love thy enemies. But in today's world you also find yourself loving unexceptional folks who are in your life through no choice of your own: the parents of your kids' friends, a former col-league who now lives on disability, gregar-ious couples you met on vacation, your rich uncle's ex-wife, and an old flame who thinks that you are the cat's meow.

You can't be too picky. Your best friend moved to Rome, your siblings live on the other coast, and many of the excit-ing people you know are too busy to stay in touch except for an occasional let's-get-together card.

No matter how caring you are, it's always a challenge to be on the receiving end of unrequited effusiveness. Try to endure gracefully the homage of a heart, though. Love is a funny thing: You don't have to like someone to love him or her dearly.

Start by standing still while accepting compliments. Don't blush. Don't act embar-rassed. Be as regal as the queen of England. By mustering as much dignity as you can

when well-wishers are lauding you, you honor their feelings and their judgment. And the next time around, when it's your turn to praise someone, you'll know how to turn the occasion into a lightsome and solicitous moment.

Next, train yourself to open all gifts big and small with resolute conviction. Don't let anything distract you as you struggle with the ribbon. If you decide to use scissors, handle them with as much dexterity as a tailor. Fold the wrapping paper and save the box. The manner in which you receive a gift is the gift you give in return.

Most important, perhaps, is to learn to accept invitations and favors without feel-ing that you are indebted as a result. You are paying your friends, acquaintances, and loved ones the greatest of all compliments by assuming that their largesse comes with no strings attached.

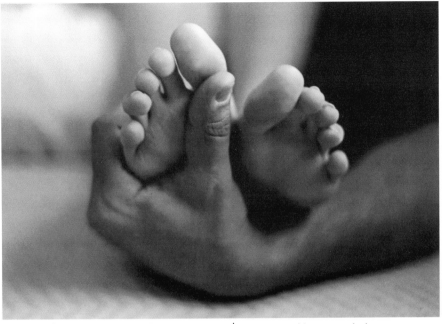

Receiving requires as much generosity as giving.

Stand firm in your refusal to believe that there is no such thing as a free lunch. Settle down in your chair. Look your host in the eye. Say "Bon appétit!"—and smile.

Guilt-free enjoyment of other people's kindness is a courageous act of faith. Never stop trusting that everyone out there is potentially as generous as you are. By accepting what's given to you moment by moment without looking over your shoulder, you keep inventing a better and better world.

Feel the Caress
of the Universe

We are all familiar with the pull of gravity, particularly when we are tired and have to get up from a comfortable chair. We feel then as if we were lifting our own dead weight from the ground.

But what would happen if instead of picturing gravity as a constant tug from under, we pictured it as a uniform embrace from above?

1. Imagine a force pressing down gently on your head and shoulders.

2. Feel it as it flows downward along your chest, back, and limbs, shaping your muscles and smoothing angles as it goes.

3. Lift your arms slowly and open your fingers to let this invisible stream caress your skin.

4. Get up like someone swimming toward the surface of a pool.

5. Rotate your body slightly on your way up to take advantage of the soft current.

6. Walk around, as if dancing under a light and soothing waterfall.

We are hugged by invisible forces.

the art of reverie

everie? It's like sing-
ing in the shower (without getting wet), doodling
(without a pad or pencil), and dancing (without moving your feet). Reverie is what happens when you
stop thinking logically and start associating freely.

Some situations in life cannot be handled by reason alone. Let's say you are supposed to give a toast
at your best friend's wedding. Or maybe you've vol-

unteered to do the decorations for a charity event. Where will you find some inspiration? In your right brain, according to neuroscience. All you need to do is put your rational left brain on hold to give your creative right brain a chance to come up with a solution.

Easier said than done. You must first locate the cerebral off switch that disconnects your cognitive ego. To find the concealed mechanism that will open the secret passage into inspiration, some people scratch their head and pull on their ears, while others rub their forehead and tug on their hair, and still others twist their mustache and stroke their beard.

With a little luck, after some fumbling for the hidden switch, the heavy bookcases in your skull will swivel as if by magic and your mental perspective will shift. You will find yourself in the whimsical land of reverie. There a stream of con-

sciousness will carry you toward some mysterious destination. Not much is required of you except to relax and go with the flow.

One of the functions of daydreaming, apart from releasing our creativity, is to curb our most restless impulses. Swept away by the serpentine current of free associations, we meander and digress. Instead of fretting and fuming, we explore foolish and pleasing alternatives as we go. We remember an old sweetheart. We fantasize about being elected president of the local school board. We wonder how much of an investment we would need to open a small antiquarian bookstore across the street from the bank.

Reverie is a gentle art. The masters of the genre are all lovable characters. Most of them are romantic poets, inspired mathematicians, absentminded professors, and scatterbrained folk heroes. Their bemused attitude and quixotic disposition gives their genius a popular dimension.

By making us less competitive, less set in our ways, less sure of ourselves, reverie allows us to explore more roundabout avenues of creativity. In this fanciful state of mind, we can try to foresee every aspect of a question, every cause and effect, every outcome, and every far-reaching consequence before deciding on the best course of action.

Only one other mammal seems capable of anticipating consequences to avert disasters in advance. Like human beings, whales have a superior intelligence and a language system made up of songs as complex and harmonious as our polkas, fugues, and minuets. Like us, whales seem to enjoy playful and solitary meditation. And like us, they are capable of making creative choices that promote peaceful resolutions.

In fact, in this domain whales are more successful than we are. The biggest creatures on earth—with the largest brains— they are also the least harmful. They act as if they are wary of their physical strength and careful not to hurt their marine environment. In all likelihood, during the last millennium whales have used their colossal mental abilities to remain benevolent in spite of the increasing dangers they face.

Maybe we, too, should try to come up with creative solutions that are expedient yet perfectly benign.

If two colleagues get into an argument, for instance, instead of trying to settle their quarrel, you diffuse their anger by making a funny non sequitur.

If a friend insists you go to a very chic restaurant—even though he doesn't have a reservation, a jacket, or a tie—you inadvertently give the taxi driver the wrong address, that of a charming little bistro downtown.

And if a child cries and nothing can comfort her, you scoop her into your arms and take her on a walk. The cadence of your footsteps, combined with the swinging of your hips and the sound of your heart, will be as soothing to both of you as the enigmatic song of a humpback vocalizing below the waves.

MODERN LAZINESS

❧

Now we know: Labor-saving devices are, in fact, time-consuming artifacts. We spend hours each day operating computers, organizers, adapters, copiers, recorders, players, printers, transmitters, receivers, and scanners. Instead of making life easier, technology makes it shorter.

Lingering in the moment is nearly impossible when every minute of the day is accounted for. There is only one solution: Don't make your life easier—and you'll make it longer.

To prolong the pleasure of being alive, try for a change to do a couple of things that demand some effort on your part. Sharpen pencils by hand. Drive a stick shift. Make your own pear jam. You'll be thrilled to discover that life feels a lot longer when you skip the shortcuts.

Reclaim your time; subvert efficiency. Whenever you have a choice, choose the more demanding of two options. Take the stairs instead of the elevator. Look up *labyrinthine* in the dictionary instead of clicking on the spell-check key. And before making up your mind, try to walk in the other person's shoes.

Call this being lazy. Go slowly when speed is the norm. A slacker by modern standards is someone who buys time in order to be able to think twice.

Prolong the pleasure of being alive.

Puzzles & Brainteasers

You need both logic and creativity to solve mental puzzles. But nothing is more fun than getting your right and left brains to work as a team. Here are four classic riddles that will challenge your common sense and poetic imagination.

1. *The Lovers:* A man and a woman are facing opposite directions. One is facing east and the other west. If they just catch a glimpse of each other, they'll fall in love. But there is a spell on them: They cannot walk, move, or turn around. How can love conquer all?

2. *Think Thin:* According to scientists, thinking burns calories. Your brain can break down fatty tissue—up to 2,000 calories a day. How is it possible?

3. *What's That?:* What is larger than the universe, deeper than time, lighter than a feather, and so delicious you can't resist it?

4. *Left/Right vs. Right/Wrong:* Let's assume that the rational left brain always gets it right, but the irrational right brain always gets it wrong. Confusing, isn't it? To find out which is which, you can only ask one question to one of the brains. What's that question?

ANSWERS: 1. They have been facing each other the whole time—thus looking in opposite directions! 2. Alas, thinking doesn't burn many calories, but your brain can motivate you to exercise and eat less. 3. Sorry, the answer is "Nothing." 4. "What would the other brain say if asked which brain it is?" The left brain will say "left brain" and the right brain will say "right brain."

"Anyone who isn't confused doesn't really understand the situation."
—Edward R. Murrow

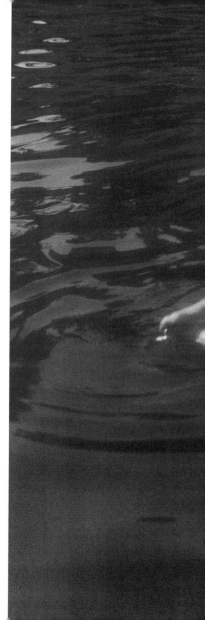

the art of serenity

herever you are, whether speeding down a highway or waiting in line at the airport, you are only one step away from serenity. That step is the glowing realization that countless human beings are smarter, wiser, gentler, nobler, faster, richer, and better-looking than you are. What a relief! The world is in good hands. You are not the highest authority of the land. You don't

have to worry about who's going to fix everything anymore.

Serenity is knowing that, regardless of how fabulous you are, you don't have to be the greatest and the best in the world. So stop torturing yourself. Ease the burden of your vanity by acknowledging the unsung heroes out there who stand head and shoulders above the crowd. Only then will you be able to savor quiet moments unencumbered by self-importance.

For openers, think of the millions of teenage girls who will grow up to become the next generation of mothers. Even though, right now, they may be staring into a mirror, bemoaning their complexion or their figure, you and I know how beautiful they will be in the eyes of their toddlers. So, whenever you feel restless, visualize these mothers-to-be: Their nascent beauty safeguards the future of humanity.

If that's not enough, picture in your mind a half-dozen boys and girls between the ages of five and seven. Marvel at their unflappable optimism. They are at that juncture in their lives where everything seems possible. Together, these six kids probably garner as much wisdom and serenity as five hundred grown-ups.

To cap it all, find peace of mind in the certainty that umpteen people will one day humble all of us with an unexpected show of generosity.

Your next-door neighbor, a cranky woman whose loud cocktail parties last way past midnight, will win a Pulitzer Prize for her courageous reportage on crime and drug wars.

An elected official, a pretentious young man who didn't get your vote, will gain your respect by passing tough legislation to protect battered women.

And don't worry. When your turn comes, you, too, will rise to the occasion.

You will find out that you are as much of a hero as anyone else. You'll champion unpopular causes and save the lives of strangers on a moment's notice.

Don't be impatient. Great people are hiding among us. Sooner or later their presence will be revealed.

In the meantime, take for granted that everyone on earth is a potential superstar; yes, everyone, from the pregnant pharmacist with her extralong nails to the tuxedoed musician boarding a crowded bus with his heavy bass.

By assuming that everyone has extraordinary talents, you let go of the lonely weight of your own loftiness. But far from being a punishing act of humility, endowing ordinary folks with qualities only you can see is a rewarding feat for your self-esteem: You may not be the greatest and the best, but you are on top of a world of your own making.

PEACEFUL RITUALS

✥

Serenity is traditionally achieved by taking pleasure in the simplest things. In every culture special rituals encourage participants to explore the wonders of the ordinary. From the daily ablutions recommended by Islam to the candlelit processions attended by Christians, small ceremonies infuse mundane activities with a sacred meaning.

The scripted nature of rituals takes away the guesswork and frees your mind to be in the moment. In addition, the simple gestures used in these ceremonies, such as washing, walking, dancing, singing, or clapping hands, keep you focused on the here and now. In this anxiety-free zone, you can experience levels of tranquillity unattainable in the real world.

The most sophisticated serenity ritual

is probably the Japanese *chanoyu*, or tea ceremony, an austere performance that combines economy of movement with exquisite attention to detail. One can hardly imagine a more choreographed way of curbing one's natural impatience.

But if rituals seem tedious to you, you can achieve the same result by practicing an enlightened form of laziness, one favored by one of the most intelligent primates on earth, our shaggy cousin the orangutan. Buddha-like creatures, these placid animals don't hunt for food like gorillas or chimps. Instead they spend hours sitting still at the tops of trees, staring at what's in front of them until they notice something they want to eat. Called "the fruit stare" by primatologists, this serene foraging method is not unlike the meditative technique used by Zen devotees.

Try the fruit stare sometime. It can work wonders when you are casting about for new ideas, looking for someone, or searching for something you lost.

If you are trying to solve a problem, stop for just thirty seconds to make room in your mind for a solution. Don't move. Gaze at the wall. Listen. Even the briefest lull can attract new thoughts.

If you are trying to find someone—whether it's a friend in a crowd or that special person out there with whom you wish to spend the rest of your life—use the same approach. Make yourself comfortable and wait. By just being there, unperturbed by the commotion, you become the most noticeable and attractive presence in a room.

But the serene gaze is by far the most effective when you are searching for a lost object: your glasses, a grocery list, or the name of a long-forgotten friend. Suspend your quest for a minute or two. Dig in your heels. Empty your lungs. Lower your lids.

Chances are, what you are looking for is hidden in plain view.

Look at the world through your eyelashes.

It's like being under a spell. The things you were looking for will soon materialize out of thin air—your glasses in your coat pocket, the grocery list under the newspaper, your friend's name in your old Rolodex. A brief moment of euphoria precedes the discovery, as if you knew all along that everything in the universe is always in the right place.

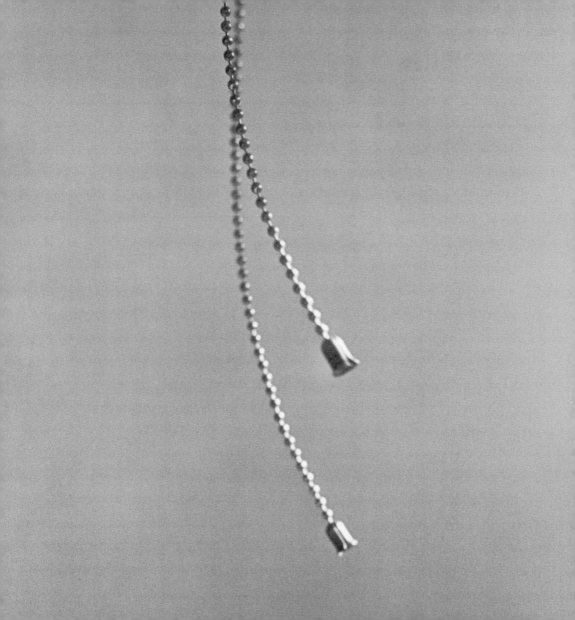

Lesson in Quiet Gratification

Doing one thing at a time—and doing it well—is a pleasure few of us can still afford. Gone are the days when you derived a lot of satisfaction from lazy afternoons knitting a sweater or from endless hours adjusting your carburetor. Don't give up, though. You can still get instant gratification from small impromptu rituals.

- Stacking newspapers neatly before throwing them away

- Keeping the pull cords of your venetian blinds untangled

- Folding your napkin carefully at the end of a great restaurant meal

- Paying for your newspaper with small change

- Stashing magazine clippings inside books on related topics

- Cleaning the pots and pans before you sit down for dinner

- Writing brief thank-you notes to writers and artists who inspire you

- Rubbing soap on old drawers so that they don't stick

- Lining up your shoes before deciding which pair to wear

- Tying a knot in plastic bags before discarding them so that they won't blow away in the wind and get stuck in trees

Small gestures bring great pleasures.

the art of prayer

hile scientists try to crack the cosmic code with the latest theory of Everything—relativity, quarks, warps, quantum fluctuations, chaos, super strings—ordinary people like you and me find simpler ways to solve the Big Riddle. We put meaning in everyday comforts: a candle flickering on an altar, the silhouette of a steeple in the distance, or the beauty of a flower languishing in a vase.

Beauty makes worshipers of the most skeptical among us.

Some things in life invite contemplation. The single long-stem rose you bought yesterday is already drooping, its heavy blossom now bowing as if in prayer. Instead of throwing it away, you keep it for a few days. In its meditative pose, the flower is a reminder of one of the greatest mysteries of all: Are we alone?

Over time, you will come up with various answers to that same nagging question. Eventually, one day it will occur to you that this endless asking is the answer you have been looking for. The fact that we have an ongoing dialogue with the universe is proof enough that there is "something" out there.

In human beings, questioning is second nature. Not only do we wonder why we can never see the hidden face of the moon, but we also wonder why there is so much poverty, injustice, and sickness on earth. It's almost as if asking questions that have no easy answers is our sacred mission in life. Even though we don't expect an instant reply, we keep praying for an explanation.

We pray on our knees, but we also pray on our feet. In churches but also in homes and offices. In silence but also in conversations. In fact, we pray whenever we are stumped by a conundrum. Physicists trying to decipher the elegant universe are praying, and so is the child engrossed in the sight of an iridescent beetle making its way across the lawn.

Imagine for a moment that instead of being a means to an end praying was its own reason for being. Indeed, in the act of prayer we celebrate a moment that would otherwise go unnoticed. To pray is to uncover an invisible gem buried under the weight of our worries. To pray is to open up to possibilities as yet unnamed.

A ten-minute conversation with a seven-year-old who is running for class president can be an uplifting moment that renews your faith in humanity.

A challenging exercise routine on a cross-trainer at the gym can reveal the spiritual dimension of the physical realm.

And a twenty-second kiss can expose heavenly perspectives.

Praying puts you in contact with

opportunities you didn't know existed. But it doesn't provide reassuring answers. It will not help you find someone or something to blame for the injustices of the world, for the foolishness of humankind, for the weakness of the flesh—and for the reason some roses only last a day.

In fact, the function of prayer is to go beyond accusations. When you join hands in prayer, you can't point the finger at anyone. The devout gesture is designed to abolish the separation between right and left, us and them, good and bad, yes and no. By closing the physical chasm between the two sides of yourself, you suspend, for a brief moment, the gnawing dualism of the rational world.

What you find out in prayer is that no one is guilty—not even yourself! Which is why prayer is so difficult. Sinners that we are, we would rather be culprits than feel powerless in the face of the unexplainable.

We would rather feel guilty than accept that in the big scheme of things we are not running the show.

An inexhaustible sense of culpability stands between us and an open-ended view of the world. If only we could give up the guilt. For being lazy. For spending too much money eating out. For forgetting birthdays. For being privileged. For not paying bills on time. For drinking too much coffee. The list is endless. The only solution is to pray. Pray in order not to agonize over the mess under the kitchen sink, the funny smell in the backseat of the family car, and the dark mildew at the bottom of the shower stall.

And if you can't pray, forgive yourself. Not making everything your fault is a form of prayer.

In a world without blame, a rose is a rose is a rose, to quote Gertrude Stein. Its fading bloom doesn't diminish its ultimate beauty. On the contrary, each withering petal reminds us of the mystifying elegance of the cosmos.

GIVING THANKS

❖

Take no blame—and no credit. Admit once and for all that you owe it all to chance. Light a candle in your heart as a show of gratitude.

Think about it: The odds against your very existence are probably a trillion to one. According to randomness experts, the chances of anything happening at a given time and place are astronomical. Your presence here now is a fluke, a gamble, a lucky accident.

First, be grateful. Even though you may not have been born with a silver spoon in your mouth, you've received many gifts from your heredity. Credit your parents and grandparents for your best qualities. Make it a little easier on yourself: Don't take full responsibility for destiny.

Next, thank the heavens for your friends and colleagues. They are the guardians of your identity. They stand by you, ready to vouch for your good character and your sterling reputation. When they return your phone calls, their voice at the other end of the line is proof that your existence is not a figment of your imagination.

Last but not least, credit your loved ones for giving you a chance to make them happy. It's a privilege not bestowed on everyone. And if you have been blessed with kids, remember what a godsend they are. Without them—and their tempering influence on your illusions—who knows what trouble you would be in today!

Give thanks for what you have received. The more you acknowledge your debt, the richer your life will be.

Hallelujah!

Show fortune your gratitude by embracing opportunities that come your way. Make the most of every chance you get to say yes by making that moment a special occasion.

The Unconditional Yes: "Absolutely!"

The Supportive Yes: "You can count on it."

The Intrepid Yes: "And how!"

The Conciliatory Yes: "But of course."

The Spirited Yes: "Believe you me!"

The Conspiratorial Yes: "Elementary, my dear Watson."

The Unflappable Yes: "No problem."

The Pragmatic Yes: "Sold!"

The Contentious Yes: "So sue me."

The French Yes: *"Mais oui!"*

The Theatrical Yes: "See how easy."

"Yes" is a moment of grace.

Savor time's hasty retreat: It's such sweet misery.

Every moment of your life can be illuminated by a ray of sunshine—the radiant beam of your attention. The beauty of each successive instant is enhanced by our perception of its brief duration. So enjoy the moment—*pluck the day*—and then let it go.

Like the words in this book, the photographs reproduced here capture the transient nature of this ephemeral glow. Bathed in natural light, the images sparkle, in suspension between glitter and shadows. A child marvels at the dappled pattern of leaves; a street awakens to the rosy fingers of dawn; and iridescent soap bubbles drift into nightfall.

As you capture the moment, you, too, will become aware of the changing light: what happens when days get shorter and shadows get longer, when clouds pass in front of the sun, when rivers and lakes shimmer in the distance.

Learn to tell time by looking at the world around you, and you won't have to check your watch to be reminded to cherish your life moment by moment.

Abbé Dinouart. *L'art de se taire.* Originally published in France by Deprez in 1771. Grenoble, France: Editions Jérome Millon, 1996.

Ackerman, Diane. *The Moon by Whale Light.* New York: Vintage Books, 1992.

Berger, John. *About Looking.* New York: Vintage Books, 1991.

Boyd, Andrew. *Life's Little Deconstruction Book.* New York: W. W. Norton & Company, 1999.

Comte-Sponville, André. *A Small Treatise on the Great Virtues.* New York: Metropolitan Books, 2001.

Dalai Lama, with Howard C. Cutler, M.D. *The Art of Happiness.* New York: Riverhead Books, 1998.

De Becker, Gavin. *The Gift of Fear.* New York: Dell Publishing, 1998.

De Botton, Alain. *The Consolations of Philosophy.* New York: Vintage Books, 2000.

Gibran, Kahlil. *Love Letters.* Oxford, England: Oneworld Publications, 2000.

Rinpoche, Sogyal. *The Tibetan Book of Living and Dying.* San Francisco: HarperCollins, 1993.

Russell, Bertrand. *The Conquest of Happiness.* New York: Liveright Publishing Corporation, 1996.

Singer, Christiane. *Où cours-tu? Ne sais-tu pas que le ciel est en toi?* Paris: Albin Michel, 2001.

The true potential of the moment is beyond our wildest imagination. All the photographs in this book were dictated to me by the way natural light reveals the preciousness of each moment. My camera sees what's hidden beneath the surface of life. I feel thankful for what my pictures teach me: to go beyond the obvious vision of the naked eye.

—ANN RHONEY

PHOTO CREDITS

Front cover: Cathy in the Sierra. *Page 2*: View from the Rainbow Room. *Page 8*: Frilly tulips in April. *Pages 10–11*: Pacific waves. *Page 14*: Mark's garage in Georgia, 2002. *Page 16*: Kathleen at the Sheas. *Pages 18–19*: Rocking chair and Maud Frizon pumps, 1983. *Page 21*: Ivory keys. *Page 24*: Wendy in Paris. *Pages 26–27*: Rhonda, David, and Dash on the Filbert Steps. *Page 28*: Becky at Seadrift, California. *Page 32*: Charlie's antique camera collection. *Pages 34–35*: After the rain in Amsterdam, 1977. *Page 36*: Door handle in Saint-Tropez, France. *Page 39*: Mosby in Normandy Village, Berkeley. *Page 41*: Charlie and Mosby. *Page 42*: Dorothy in Washington. *Pages 44–45*: Allyson and Elizabeth. *Page 47*: Fountain in Vigeland Park, Oslo, Norway, 1995. *Page 50*: Pond in Golden Gate Park, San Francisco. *Pages 52–* *53*: Becky and Doug on Stinson Beach. *Page 54*: Railroad crossing in Alviso, California, 1985. *Page 58*: The San Remo from the Excelsior Hotel, New York. *Pages 60–61*: Playing footsie on the Upper East Side. *Page 65*: Soothing ritual. *Page 66*: Hannah in St. Helena, California. *Pages 68–69*: Still life with postcards. *Page 73*: Stairwell rue de Grenelle, Paris, France. *Page 74*: Lily in Niagara Falls. *Pages 76–77*: Hannah, July Fourth weekend. *Page 81*: Virginia Coigney's apples in West Redding, Connecticut, 1990. *Page 82*: Dancing chains. *Pages 84–85*: View from Telegraph Hill, San Francisco. *Page 86 and back cover*: A perfect rose on New Year's Day, 1990. *Page 90*: Indian Summer with Becky. *Page 92*: Becky and Doug at sunset. *Page 94*: Owen at home on Newburg Street.